P O W E R P A C K

POWERPACK

Play on words

Interactive Bible stories

Kevin
Mayhew

With special thanks to Peter, Chris and Nick Jackson
who have written this collection of interactive Bible stories

First published in 2000 by
KEVIN MAYHEW LTD
Buxhall
Stowmarket
Suffolk IP14 3BW

0 1 2 3 4 5 6 7 8 9

ISBN 1 84003 623 0
Catalogue No 1500385

Cover design by Jonathan Stroulger
Illustrated by Sally-Anne Norman
Edited by Helen Elliot
Typeset by Elisabeth Bates
Printed and bound in Great Britain

CONTENTS

INTRODUCTION

This book contains thirty-four interactive dramas based on popular Bible stories. These have been used extensively in Powerpack meetings and have proved to be an enjoyable and successful way of reinforcing Bible stories. As the name suggests, everybody is involved in miming the actions to a given story. An important part of the appeal of the dramas is the humorous play on words. Although it is possible for one person to read the story and mime the actions at the same time, we have found it easier to have two people involved – one to read the story and one to do the actions.

The most obvious use of these dramas is to repeat and reinforce a Bible story which has already been told in some other way. However, they may also be used to reinforce a particular theme and for this purpose we have suggested some relevant teaching points at the beginning of each script. In such situations, the primary story for the meeting may not be that of the interactive drama, in which case we suggest you choose a drama based on a story the children know well or the play on words can leave them a little confused!

It should also be noted that very young children won't understand the play on words and, as this could lead to their misunderstanding the Bible story, some of the actions may need to be changed to give a more literal interpretation.

As well as using these dramas in children's meetings and school assemblies and the like, they can be very effective in an all-age context, since they are a good way of involving adults and children together. Adults seem to enjoy them as much as children! As with anything else, 'familiarity breeds contempt', so be careful not to overuse them.

When writing these scripts it hasn't always been easy to explain exactly the actions and expressions we have used, since sometimes it is better to complete the sense of a particular phrase and so combine the suggested actions into one longer movement. We would therefore encourage you always to prepare the dramas beforehand, deciding where to pause and which actions to join up, if any. You may also find that there are too many actions and you will need to cut some, or you may want to change some of the actions to suit your own situation or even add extra ones of your own.

In the scripts, *** following a word indicates an action, which is explained in the brackets. If the starred word appears later in the script, there is no explanation given but obviously repeat the same action. As you read the scripts you will see that we have used some standard actions and although you will soon become familiar with these, we felt it necessary to indicate them throughout so that each script can stand on its own. Occasionally the same word, which appears in several of the scripts, may be given a different action – that is to help counter predictability and to add variety.

We trust that you and your children will enjoy using these dramas. Have fun!

ABRAHAM AND SARAH

Genesis 12-21

Teaching point
• *God always keeps his promises*

A long, long, lo . . . ng *** *(say 'long' slowly and stretch out arms)* time ago *** *(look at watch)* there lived a man called Abraham *** *(stroke beard)* and his wife Sarah *** *(mime two kisses)*. They both loved God *** *(point upwards)* very much and lived good lives *** *(thumbs up)*.

One day God *** told Abraham *** to take his wife *** and his servants *** *(bow head several times with hands together)* and leave his country and go to a new land *** *(aeroplane landing)* that he would show them. God *** promised *** *(Cub/Brownie salute)* Abraham *** that he was going to bless *** *(thumbs up)* him and that he would be the father of a great *** *(indicate large size)* nation. So *** *(sew)* Abraham *** obeyed God *** and eventually after a very long *** journey the family arrived in Canaan *** *(mime caning!)*.

Some time *** passed *** *(move head quickly from one side to the other)* and again God *** promised *** Abraham that he was going to be the father of a great *** nation. He was going to have a son! But how could this be? *** *(shrug shoulders)*. Abraham and his wife, Sarah ***, did not have any children *** *(indicate decreasing heights)* and Sarah *** was far too old *** *(mime old person)* to have a baby *** *(suck thumb)* now. When Sarah *** heard God's *** promise *** she laughed *** *(hilarious silent laughter)*. How could an old *** lady like her have a baby ***?

But God *** kept his promise *** and when Abraham was 100 *** *(show 10 x 10 fingers)* and Sarah *** was 90 *** *(show 9 x 10 fingers)* the baby *** was born *** *(baby cry!)*. He was called Isaac which means 'he laughs' ***, because Abraham's *** wife, Sarah ***, had laughed *** when she had heard God's *** promise ***. But how pleased *** *(cheesy grin)* they were with their special baby boy ***.

ADAM AND EVE

Genesis 2:15-3:24

Teaching points
- temptation
- disobedience

Adam *** *(boys march left, right, on the spot)* and Eve *** *(girls march left, right, on the spot)* lived a long, lo . . . ng *** *(say 'long' slowly and stretch out arms)* time *** *(look at watch)* ago, in a beautiful garden *** *(kiss fingers, Italian-chef style!)*. Everything was really good *** *(thumbs up!)* and God *** *(point upwards)* walked *** *(walk on the spot)* in the garden *** and talked *** *(talking action with hand)* with Adam *** and Eve *** every day.

They were very happy *** *(hilarious silent laughter)* in the garden ***, but God *** had told them *** *(wag finger in telling-off fashion)* that there was one thing *** *(show one finger)* they must not do *** *(shake head)* – eat the fruit *** *(eat fruit noisily, rub tummy)* of the tree *** *(make an unusual tree shape!)* in the middle of the garden ***. If they did then they would die *** *(die dramatically with suitable sound effects)*.

One day, a serpent *** *(wiggle arm, say 'ssssss'!)* came and told Eve *** it was OK *** *(thumbs up)* to eat the fruit ***, and that they would not die ***. So *** *(sew)* she picked the fruit *** *(pick fruit from tree)* and ate it ***. Then she gave some *** *(give to someone)* to Adam *** who ate it *** as well.

Soon God *** came into the garden ***. He said, 'Where are you *** *(look around, hand across eyes)*, Adam ***? Where are you ***, Eve ***?' Adam *** and Eve *** were hiding *** *(turn away, arms over head)*. They felt ashamed *** *(cover face with hands)* and guilty *** *(fearful, biting nails)*. They knew they had done wrong and they didn't want to see *** *(look through binoculars)* God ***.

God *** knew *** *(point to side of head)* what they had done and was very sad *** *(cry dramatically)*. Everything that was so good *** was now so bad *** *(thumbs down)*. He would have to put Adam *** and Eve *** out of the garden now *** *(point to one side)* and no more would they be close friends *** *(join own hands together in front of you)*. What was he going to do now *** *(shrug shoulders)*?

DANIEL IN THE LIONS' DEN

Daniel 6

Teaching points
- only one God
- stand firm
- importance of prayer
- God saves

There was once a man called Daniel *** *(left, right, march on the spot)*. When Daniel *** was only about 14 *** *(show 14 fingers)* he was taken prisoner *** *(wrists tied together)* to a land far away *** *(hand across eyes, peer into the distance)* called Babylon *** *(point to the side)*. But God *** *(point upwards)* looked after Daniel *** and protected him *** *(shielding/guarding action)*.

After a short time *** *(indicate short measure and look at watch)* Daniel *** became a ruler *** *(make shape of a drawing ruler)* in Babylon ***. He served *** *(serving action)* King Nebuchadnezzar *** *(indicate crown)* and told him what his dreams meant *** *(head on hands and snore!)*. But Daniel *** loved God *** *(hug self and point to God)*. He thought *** *(point to side of head)* God *** was the greatest! *** *(thumbs up)* – the only one *** *(show 1 finger)*, true *** *(cross heart)* God ***. So *** *(sew)*, three times *** *(show 3 fingers)* every day Daniel *** prayed *** *(praying hands)* – he talked to God ***.

As time went on *** *(circle watch while moving arm along)* Daniel *** also served King Darius *** and became a very important *** *(pull imaginary braces!)* leader *** *(salute)* in Babylon ***. Because of this, some of the other leaders *** *(several salutes)* who were very wicked and evil *** *(wring hands while pulling an evil face)* became jealous *** *(make suitable sneering expression!)* of Daniel *** and plotted *** *(thoughtful/scheming action)* to get rid of him *** *(slit throat and drop head!)*.

They went to the king *** with an idea *** *(point to side of head and eyes light up)*. No one was to pray *** to any god or man except to the king *** for 30 days *** (show 3 x 10 fingers). If they did they would be thrown *** (throwing action) into a den of lions *** (pounce and roar!). This pleased *** (indicate smile on face) the king *** and he said OK *** (thumbs up!), and this law was written down *** (write in exaggerated style and point downwards). The wicked *** leaders *** knew that Daniel *** prayed *** three times *** each day, and so this would cause a problem for him *** (look worried/puzzled/thoughtful). What would he do *** (shrug shoulders)?

When he heard the news *** (cup hand around ear), Daniel *** went to his house *** (make house shape), went upstairs to his room *** (go up stairs), knelt down *** (bend knees) and prayed *** to God *** at his open window *** (open window), just as he had always done. The wicked *** leaders *** were watching *** (peer, squint evilly!), and as soon as they saw *** (saw wood) Daniel *** praying *** they went to the king *** and told him that Daniel *** must be thrown *** to the lions *** and die *** (die dramatically)!

The king *** was very upset *** (exaggerated crying). He loved *** Daniel *** but a law, once written down ***, could not be broken *** (SNAP!/mime breaking action). So *** he gave the OK *** for Daniel *** to be thrown *** into the lions' *** den, but he hoped that God *** would save him *** (football save!). That night he could not eat *** (eating action) or sleep *** (head on hands and snore) because he was so worried *** (look worried, biting fingernails).

The next morning King Darius *** hurried *** (run on the spot) to the lions' den ***. He called out, 'Daniel, has your God saved you?' *** (Repeat). Daniel *** replied that God *** had saved *** him, and had sent an angel *** (indicate halo, saying 'ping') to shut the lions' mouths *** (roar and then clap hands together crocodile-style!).

Then King Darius ordered that Daniel *** was to be pulled *** (pull as in tug of war) up out of the lions' den ***, and that all the wicked *** leaders *** who had schemed and plotted *** should be thrown *** to the lions *** instead.

Also *** (all sew) the king *** wrote a letter *** to all the people in his kingdom, saying that they must now worship *** (bow down) the only one *** true *** God *** – the God *** who had saved *** Daniel ***. HOORAY (all cheer)!

DAVID AND GOLIATH

1 Samuel 17

Teaching points
- trust in God
- God's power working in us

There was once a boy *** *(indicate short person)* called David *** *(left, right, march on the spot)*. He looked after the sheep *** *(baa!)*, and was the smallest *** *(crouch down)* member of the family. Now David *** loved *(hug yourself)* God *** *(point upwards)* and he believed *(point to side of head)* that God *** was the greatest *** *(thumbs up)*!

One day, his father sent *** *(apply perfume behind ears!)* David *** on a lo . . . ng *** *(say 'long' slowly and stretch out arms)* journey, with food *** *(exaggerate eating and rub tummy)* for his brothers *** *(indicate increasing heights)*, who were fighting *** *(pretend to fight)* in King Saul's *** *(place crown on head)* army *** *(tap arm)*.

As he came near *** *(lean forward)* he saw *** *(saw wood)* in the distance *** *(peer forward, hand across eyes)* a giant *** *(say 'GIANT' in a deep voice)* of a man. His name was Goliath *** *(beat on chest gorilla-style, making a Tarzan call)*. Goliath *** was laughing *** *(evil laugh in deep voice)*. 'Who will come and fight me ***?' he roared *** *(ROAR!)* in a loud voice *** *(shout 'VOICE')*. But all of King Saul's *** soldiers *** *(stand to attention)* were hiding *** *(turn away with arms over head)* in their tents *** *(look tense!)*

Shortly *** *(indicate short distance or short person)* after this, when David *** had given his brothers *** the food ***, he went to see *** *(look through binoculars)* King Saul *** and offered to fight *** Goliath ***. 'You're only a boy!' *** *(suck thumb!)* said King Saul ***, but David *** said, 'God *** will help me.'

So *** *(sew)* David *** took five *** *(show 5 fingers)* stones from the stream *** *(indicate running water)*, and went out to fight *** Goliath ***. Goliath *** laughed *** when he saw *** David ***, but David shouted, 'You come against me with sword *** *(fight with sword)* and spear *** *(throw down spear)* and javelin *** *(throw javelin a long way)*, but I come against you in the name of the Lord almighty *** *(point upwards)*.'

Then David *** put a stone in his sling *** *(arm in a sling!)* and spun it round and round and round *** *(spin sling round and round or turn round repeatedly on the spot)*. It flew through the air *** *(aeroplane flying)* and struck *** *(slap fist into palm of other hand)* Goliath *** on the forehead *** *(show four fingers and slap forehead)* and killed him *** *(die dramatically)*! He fell to the ground with a loud thud *** *(shout 'THUD!' and hit palm with fist)*. God *** had helped David *** to defeat *** *(cut off feet! Or hold nose and say 'pooh'!)* Goliath ***. HOORAY *(all cheer)*!

ELIJAH AND THE PROPHETS OF BAAL

1 Kings 19:20-40

Teaching point
• only one true God

A lo . . . ng, long *** *(say 'long' slowly while stretching out arms)* time ago, there lived a very wicked *** *(wring hands while pulling an evil face)* king *** *(indicate crown)*. His name was Ahab, and he was king *** of Israel. King Ahab *** had a wife called Queen Jezebel *** *(indicate 'wavy' crown, saying 'ding'!)*, who was much more *** *(indicate large shape)* wicked and evil *** than the king ***. She built *** *(mime building action)* statues *** *(be a statue)*, called idols, made of wood *** *(knock on head!)*, iron *** *(mime ironing)*, brass *** *(blow a trumpet!)* and even gold and silver *** *(point to a ring or other jewellery)*.

Queen Jezebel *** worshipped *** *(bowing down action)* these statues *** and refused to worship *** the one *** *(show 1 finger)*, true *** *(cross heart)* God *** *(point upwards)* of Israel. It wasn't long *** before King Ahab *** also *** *(all sew!)* began to worship *** the statues *** of wood ***, iron ***, brass *** and gold and silver ***.

The two *** *(show 2 fingers)* most important *** *(look important, holding lapels)* statues *** were called Baal *** *(bleat 'Baaaal'!)* and Asherah *** *(sneeze – 'Ashoo rah!')* and Queen Jezebel *** appointed *** *(point a few times)* prophets to look after *** *(hand across eyes peering into distance)* them. These prophets were wicked people *** too *** *(show 2 fingers)*.

God *** was angry *** *(pull angry face)* with King Ahab *** and Queen Jezebel *** and sent *** *(scent behind ears!)* his prophet Elijah *** *(shout 'The Lord is God')* to him with a message. Elijah *** told the king

*** that there would not be any rain *** (indicate falling rain) for two *** or three *** (show 3 fingers) years. During this time *** (look at watch) God *** looked after *** Elijah ***, until in the third *** year, he sent *** him back *** (touch back) to King Ahab ***.

Elijah *** told the king *** to order all the people of Israel to go up *** (aeroplane take off!) onto Mount Carmel *** (indicate mountain) as well as 450 *** (show 4 fingers, then 10 x 10 really quickly and finally 5 x 10) prophets of Baal *** and the 400 *** (show 4 fingers then 10 x 10) prophets of the goddess Asherah ***, who served Queen Jezebel ***.

On Mount Carmel *** Elijah *** told the people to bring two *** bulls *** (show horns, head down and 'moo' – twice!). He told the prophets of Baal *** to call on their god to send fire *** (make the sound of wind and flame shapes) to burn up the bull *** they were offering.

So *** (sew) all day the prophets of Baal *** prayed to their statue god ***. They shouted, 'Baal, answer us' *** (shout 'Baal, answer us') but nothing happened. Elijah *** told them to shout louder *** (shout louder) because perhaps their god was day-dreaming *** (look dreamy!) or even asleep *** (head on hands, snoring). So they shouted even louder, 'Baal, answer us' ***. They even cut themselves with knives and daggers *** (mime cutting body). But guess what? Nothing happened.

Then Elijah *** told the people to pour *** (pour from large jars) water all over the bull *** and the wood *** until everything was dripping wet *** (shake off water). After this, Elijah *** prayed *** to God *** and God *** answered and sent *** down fire *** to burn up the offering. The people of Israel were amazed *** (look amazed) and turned back *** (touch back) to God ***. They were really sorry *** (cry dramatically) that they had worshipped *** Queen Jezebel's *** statues *** – the gods of Baal *** and Asherah ***.

NB: Elijah's name means 'The Lord is God'.

___ ELISHA AND THE SYRIAN ARMY ___

2 Kings 6:8-23

Teaching points
- God's ways different from ours
- power of love and forgiveness

The king of Syria was at war *** *(box!)* with Israel. He consulted his officers *** *(salute)* and chose a place *** *(make fish movement!)* to set up his camp. But Elisha *** *(left, right, march on the spot)* sent word to the king *** *(indicate crown)* of Israel, warning him not *** *(wag finger)* to go near the place *** because the Syrians *** *(make a silly face or action – reader says, 'Syria, not sillier!')* were waiting in ambush *** *(make bush shape!)* there.

So *** *(sew)* the king *** of Israel warned *** the men who lived in the place *** and they were on guard *** *(sentry)*. This happened several times *** *(indicate watch)*. The king *** of Syria *** became very upset *** *(exaggerated crying)* over this. He called his officers *** and asked, 'Which one of you is on the side *** *(indicate side of body)* of the king *** of Israel?'

'No one is, Your Majesty *** *(bow)*. The prophet Elisha *** tells the king *** of Israel everything you say, even in the privacy of your own room.'

'Find out where he is,' the king *** ordered, 'and I will capture him *** *(hug self)*.'

When he was told that Elisha *** was in Dothan, he sent a large *** *(indicate large shape)* force there with horses *** *(clip-clop x 2)* and chariots *(reins/whip)*. They reached the town at night *** *(knight/visor/lance)* and surrounded it *** *(arms in circle)*.

Early next morning *** *(cock-a-doodle doo!)*, Elisha's *** servant got up *** *(upward movement)* and saw *** *(saw wood)* the Syrian troops with their horses *** and chariots ***, surrounding *** the town. He went back *** *(touch back)* to Elisha *** and said, 'We are doomed! *** *(oh, no!)*. What shall we do?'

'Don't be afraid *** *(look terrified, biting fingernails)*,' said Elisha, *** 'we have more on our side *** than they have on theirs.'

Then he prayed *** *(hands together)*, 'O Lord *** *(point upwards)*, open his eyes and let him see *** *(indicate sea)*.' The Lord *** answered his prayer ***. The servant looked up *** *(look up)* and saw *** the hillside covered with horses *** and chariots *** of fire *** *(whoosh!)* all round *** Elisha ***.

When the Syrians *** attacked, Elisha *** prayed ***, 'O Lord, *** strike *** *(strike a match)* these men blind *** *(cover eyes)*.' The Lord *** answered his prayer *** and struck *** them blind ***. Then Elisha *** went to them and said, 'You are on the wrong *** *(cross)* road, this is not *** the town you are looking for *** *(look through binoculars)*. Follow me and I will lead you to the man you are after.' He led them into the city of Samaria. Elisha *** prayed ***: 'Open their eyes, Lord *** and let them see ***.' The Lord *** answered his prayer *** and he restored their sight and they saw *** they were inside Samaria.

When the king *** of Israel saw *** the Syrians *** he asked Elisha ***, 'Shall I kill *** *(stab)* them, sir?'

'No,' answered Elisha ***, 'you would not *** kill *** soldiers *** you had captured *** in combat ***. Give them something to eat *** *(munch, munch!)* and drink *** *(slurp, slurp!)* and let them return to their king ***.' So *** the king *** of Israel gave them lots to eat *** and drink *** and sent them back *** to the king *** of Syria ***.

From that time *** the Syrians *** stopped *** *(mime stop sign)* raiding the land of Israel. The Israelites were well pleased *** *(cheesy grin)*!

___ GIDEON AND THE MIDIANITES ___

Judges 7

Teaching points
- obeying God's instructions
- working together

One day Gideon *** *(salute)* and his men got up early *** *(stretch, yawn)* and camped beside the Spring of Harad *** *(boing! springing up action)*. The Midianites *** *(BOO!)* were in the valley *** *(make valley shape)* below *** *(point downwards)*. The Lord *** *(point upwards)* said to Gideon ***, 'The men you have are too many. They might think *** *(point to side of head)* they've won *** *(show 1 finger)* by themselves. Announce to everyone *** *(point to everyone)* that anyone who is afraid *** *(look terrified, biting nails)* should go back home *** *(point to one side).'* So *** *(sew)*, twenty *** *(show 20 fingers)* thousand went back *** *(turn away, touching back)* and ten *** *(show 10 fingers)* thousand stayed *** *(turn to face audience)*.

Then the Lord *** said to Gideon ***, 'You still have too many men. Take them to the water *** *(mime water)* and I will separate *** *(mime a dividing action)* them for you.' Gideon *** took his men down to the water *** and there the Lord *** said, 'Separate *** everyone who laps up *** *(lapping action)* the water *** with his tongue *** *(waggle tongue!)* from everyone who gets down on his knees *** *(kneel or bend knees)* to drink *** *(straighten up, GLUG!).'* There were only three *** *(show 3 fingers)* hundred men who lapped *** the water *** with their tongue ***. All the rest were sent back *** while the three *** hundred stayed ***.

All this time *** *(look at watch)*, the Midianites *** were below them *** in the valley ***. Gideon *** separated his men into three *** *(show 3 fingers)* groups, and he gave each man a trumpet *** *(blow trumpets)* and a jar with a torch *** *(shine torch around)* inside it. He said, 'Watch me *** *(look at watch)* and do what I *** *(point to eye)* do. When my group and I *** blow our trumpets *** then you blow your trumpets *** and shout "For the Lord *** and for Gideon ***" *(shout FOR THE LORD *** AND FOR GIDEON ***)*.' Gideon *** and his men marched *** *(march on spot)* to the edge of the camp just before midnight *** *(12 dongs!)*. Then they blew their trumpets *** and broke the jars *** *(shout CRASH!)*, they held up their torches *** *(arm up)* and their trumpets *** and shouted *** *(shout FOR THE LORD *** AND FOR GIDEON ***)*.

The whole enemy army *** *(point to arm)* ran away *** *(run on the spot)*, yelling for help *(shout 'HELP!')* and attacked each other with their swords *** *(mime sword fight)*. The Lord *** had helped Gideon *** to defeat *** *(point to feet!)* the enemy *** HOORAY *(all cheer)*!

JESUS WALKS ON THE WATER

Matthew 14:22-33; Mark 6:45-51; John 6:15-21

Teaching point
- Jesus is Lord over nature

There is a story *** *(open book as in charades)* about Jesus *** *(use deaf signing action, i.e. touch nail prints in palm of each hand with opposite middle finger)* feeding *** *(mime eating)* five *** *(show 5 fingers)* thousand people *** *(point round to audience)* with only five *** loaves and two *** *(show 2 fingers)* fish *** *(indicate fish swimming)*.

Well, straight *** *(stand up straight)* after this, Jesus *** told his disciples to climb *** *(mime climbing)* into their boat *** *(make boat shape)* and go over *** *(arm over!)* to the other side *** *(indicate side of body)* of the lake *** *(indicate wavy water)*. Then Jesus *** went up *** *(aeroplane take-off)* onto the mountainside *** *(indicate mountain and then side of body)* to pray *** *(praying hands)*.

When evening came the boat *** was in the middle of the lake *** and Jesus *** was alone on land. He saw *** *(saw wood)* the disciples straining at the oars *** *(strained rowing!)*, because the wind was blowing *** *(blow)* hard against them *** *(push hands slowly out in front of you)*. In the middle of the night, Jesus *** went out to them walking *** *(walk on the spot)* on the lake ***. When the disciples saw *** him, they thought *** *(point to side of head)* he was a ghost *** *(make ghostly noise)* and they were terrified *** *(look terrified, biting nails)*.

Jesus *** shouted to them, 'Take courage *** *(look brave, stand strong)*! It is I *** *(point to eye!)*. Don't be afraid *** *(shield face with hands)*.'

Then Peter *** *(left, right, march on the spot)* said, 'Lord, if it's you, tell me to come *** *(beckon)* to you on the water ***.'

Jesus *** said, 'Come ***'.

So *** *(sew)* Peter *** climbed *** out of the boat *** and walked *** on the water *** to Jesus ***. But when he saw *** the waves *** *(make large wave shapes)* and heard *** *(cup hand round ear)* the wind ***, he was afraid *** and began to sink *** *(sink down)*. He shouted out, 'Lord, save me *** *(Shout out 'Lord, save me')*!'

Jesus *** pulled *** *(pull as in tug of war)* Peter *** up out of the water ***. 'Why did you doubt?' he said. Then they both climbed *** back *** *(touch back)* into the boat *** and the wind *** and the waves *** died down *** *(die down!)*.

All the disciples were amazed *** *(look amazed, drop jaw)* and afraid ***, too *** *(show 2 fingers)*. They worshipped *** *(bowing down action)* Jesus *** and said, 'Truly you are the Son of God *** *(point upwards)*'.

JOHN THE BAPTIST'S BIRTH

Luke 1:5-25, 57-80

Teaching points
- dedication to God
- answer to prayer

In the time *** (*look at watch*) of Herod *** (*BOO!*), the king *** (*indicate crown*) of Judah, there was a priest *** (*hands together, bowing head*) named Zechariah. He and his wife *** (*hug self or blow a kiss!*) Elizabeth were descendants *** (*indicate decreasing heights*) of Aaron *** (*mime 'hair on'!*).

Zechariah and Elizabeth loved *** (*hug self*) God *** (*point upwards*) and always did what was right *** (*tick!*). But there was one thing *** (*show 1 finger*) which always made them sad *** (*look sad or cry dramatically*) – they had no children *** (*indicate decreasing heights*), and now they were very old *** (*mime old person*).

One day when Zechariah was serving *** (*tennis serve*) as priest *** in the temple *** (*make spire shape or point to own temple!*), the angel Gabriel *** (*indicate halo, saying 'ping'*) came and stood before him. When he saw *** (*saw wood*) the angel *** Zechariah was confused *** (*look confused*) and frightened *** (*look afraid, biting nails*).

'Don't be afraid ***,' said the angel ***. 'God *** has heard *** (*cup hand round ear*) your prayer *** (*praying hands*). Your wife *** Elizabeth is going to have a baby *** (*cry like a baby or suck thumb*) and you must call him John. You will be very happy *** (*hilarious silent laughter*). Many people will be happy *** because of his birth. John will be a very important *** (*look important holding lapels*) man for the Lord ***. He will never drink *** (*glug!*) alcoholic *** (*hic!*) drink ***, but he will be filled with the Holy Spirit even as a baby ***. He will help people turn *** (*spin round*) back *** (*touch back*) to God *** and be ready for when Jesus *** (point upwards or use deaf signing action, i.e. touch nail prints on palms of each hand with middle finger) comes.'

Zechariah was amazed *** (gasp, drop jaw) and said, 'How do I know this is really true *** (cross heart)? My wife *** and I are far too old *** to have a baby ***.'

The angel Gabriel *** said, 'It is true ***, but, because you have not believed, you will be struck *** (clock striking or hit self) dumb (finger on lips) until the time *** (look at watch) comes for the baby to be born *** (baby cry).'

And so *** (sew) it was. Zechariah became dumb *** and could only speak with sign language *** (mime signing) until the baby was born ***. Then the people asked Zechariah what the baby *** was to be called. As soon as Zechariah wrote down *** (mime writing and duck down) the name John, he was able to speak again.

Zechariah and Elizabeth were both very happy *** with their special baby ***. Soon he would grow up *** (grow up) to be a mighty *** (flex muscles) man of God ***.

JONAH

Teaching points
- disobedience
- God's judgement and mercy

There was once a man called Jonah *** *(left, right, march on the spot)*. Jonah *** was a prophet, a man who brought messages from God *** *(point upwards)* to the people *** *(take 'letters' from God and deal them out to the audience)*. One day, God *** told Jonah *** to go to Nineveh *** *(point towards the right)*, and tell the people there *** *(wag finger as in telling off)* that because they were so wicked and evil *** *(wring hands while pulling an evil face)*, he was going to destroy the city *** *(thump fist on open palm)* in forty days *** *(show 10 fingers 4 times)*. But Jonah *** was frightened *** *(look terrified, biting nails)* and set off in the opposite direction *** *(point towards the left)* towards Joppa.

There he boarded a ship sailing for Spain *** *(in style of Spanish dancer and saying 'OLE!')*. But the Lord sent a strong wind *** *(flex arm muscles and blow)*, over the sea *** *(look through binoculars)*. The wind came up *** *(raise arms upwards)*, the waves came up *** *(raise arms upwards)* and their lunch came up *** *(pretend to vomit)*! The sailors *** *(sing Popeye theme tune while climbing the rigging!)* were terrified *** and cried out for help *** *(Shout 'HELP!')* to their own gods. They threw *** *(mime 'through' – pass finger through hole made by forefinger and thumb of other hand)* cargo *** *(drive a car)* overboard to lighten *** *(indicate flashing lights with hands)* the ship.

All this time *** *(look at watch)* Jonah *** was asleep *** *(head on hands and snore!)* in the ship's hold *** *(hug yourself)*. The captain *** *(salute)* found him and said, 'Get up and pray *** *(hands together)* to your God *** for help ***'. The sailors *** said to Jonah ***, 'Who are you? Where do you come from?' Jonah *** told them he was running away *** *(run on the spot)* from God *** and the only way to stop *** *(hand signal for stop)* the storm was to throw him *** *(throw overboard)* into the sea ***. So *** *(sew)* that's just what the sailors *** did.

But God *** sent a lar . . . ge *** *(say 'large' slowly, moving hands outwards to indicate size)* fish to swallow *** *(gulp!)* Jonah ***. He was inside the lar . . . ge *** fish for three *** *(show 3 fingers)* days and nights. Jonah *** prayed *** to the Lord ***, 'Please save me and I will go to Nineveh ***'. So *** God *** commanded the lar . . . ge *** fish to spew *** Jonah *** up on the beach. Again, God *** said, 'Go to Nineveh ***'. Jonah *** obeyed and went to Nineveh ***.

When he got there, Jonah *** told the people *** that because they were so wicked and evil *** God *** was going to destroy the city *** in forty days ***. The people were very sorry *** *(cry dramatically)* and decided to change their ways *** *(turn round on the spot)*. When God *** saw *** *(saw wood)* that they were sorry *** he changed his mind *** *(indicate circular motion at side of head)* and did not punish them or destroy the city ***. HOORAY *(all cheer)*!

JOSHUA AT JERICHO

Joshua 6

Teaching point
• following God's instructions gives victory

Joshua *** (left, right, march on the spot) was brave *** (hands on hips, push out chest) and strong *** (flex arm muscles). He was God's *** (point upwards) man, and the leader *** (salute) of God's *** army *** (point to arm), the Israelites. God *** spoke to Joshua ***, and told him he was going to help him capture *** (hug self) the city *** (sing 'City, city . . .' football-style!) of Jericho *** (make a circle with arms), with its king *** (crown on head) and all its brave *** soldiers *** (say 'LEFT, RIGHT, LEFT, RIGHT').

God *** said to Joshua ***, the leader *** of the Israelites, 'March round *** (march round in a circle on the spot) the city *** of Jericho *** for seven days *** (show 7 fingers). On the seventh day the priests *** (hands together bowing head) must blow *** (blow with mouth) their trumpets *** (trumpet sounds), sounding one lo . . . ng *** (say 'long' slowly) note *** (sing 'LAH!'). As soon as they hear it *** (cup hand round ear), all the men must give a loud shout *** (shout 'SHOUT!') and the city *** of Jericho *** will collapse *** (clap crocodile-style!).'

At daybreak *** (snapping action/sound), they got up *** (indicate rising) to do what God *** had said. An advance guard *** (stand to attention) went ahead *** (point to head) of the army *** and the priests *** blew *** the trumpets ***.

The next day the same thing happened – and so on for six *** (show 6 fingers) days. On the seventh day *** (show 7 fingers), they got up *** at daybreak ***, and marched round *** the city *** of Jericho *** seven times ***.

On the seventh *** time *** (look at watch) round *** (turn round), Joshua ***, the leader *** of God's *** army ***, gave the order. The priests *** blew *** the trumpets ***. As soon as the men heard *** the sound *** (PING!) they gave a loud shout ***, and the walls collapsed ***. The army *** went up *** the hill, into the city *** of Jericho ***, and captured *** it. HOORAY (all cheer)!

MARY AND MARTHA

Luke 10:38-42

Teaching point
• lovers of God before workers

One day Jesus *** *(point upwards)* and his followers *** *(walk on the spot)* went to the house *** *(make roof shape)* of Mary *** *(lightly stamp left foot)* and Martha *** *(lightly stamp right foot)*. Mary *** and Martha *** were really pleased *** *(cheesy grin)* to see *** *(indicate sea or look through binoculars)* Jesus *** and his followers ***. Mary *** sat down *** *(mime sitting down)* with Jesus *** and listened *** *(cup hand round ear)* to his teaching.

Meanwhile, Martha *** was busy *** *(act busily)* in the house ***. She was probably baking bread *** *(knead dough)* and cooking the dinner *** *(mime cooking at the stove)*. Perhaps the house *** was a tip *** *(mime tipping something up!)* and so she was cleaning up *** *(mime sweeping, dusting, etc.)* or perhaps she was laying *** *(lay an egg)* the table *** *(mime table shape)*.

All this time *** *(look at watch)* Mary *** was listening *** to Jesus ***. Martha *** began to get annoyed *** *(look annoyed, fold arms)*. 'Mary *** should be helping me *** *(point to self)*,' she thought. 'It's not fair *** *(stamp foot angrily)*! I'm just so *** *(sew)* busy *** , while she's out there doing nothing *** *(spread out hands angrily)*. Why should I do all the work *** *(hurriedly make dough, cook dinner, clean floor, etc.)*? It's not fair ***!'

So *** Martha *** went to Jesus *** and said, 'I'm so *** busy ***. It's not fair ***! Tell Mary *** to come and help me ***.'

'Martha ***, Martha ***,' said Jesus ***, 'Why are you so busy ***? You are worried *** *(look worried, biting fingernails)* and upset *** *(cry dramatically!)* about so *** many things. Mary *** has chosen the best way of all.'

I think Jesus *** wanted Martha *** to relax *** *(relax!)*, stop being so *** busy *** and spend some time *** with him. Do you *** *(point to audience)*?

__ MOSES AND THE BURNING BUSH __

Exodus 3:1-17

Teaching point
• God's calling

One day Moses *** *(mow the lawn!)* was looking after *** *(hand across eyes, peering ahead)* Jethro's *** *(pretend to throw something)* sheep *** *(baa!)*. Jethro *** was Moses' *** father-in-law. Moses *** decided to take Jethro's *** sheep *** to the west side *** *(point to the west and then indicate side of body)* of the desert. There he came to Sinai *** *(sign signature and point to eye!)*, the mountain *** *(indicate mountain)* of God *** *(point upwards)*.

At Sinai *** the angel *** *(indicate halo and say 'ping!')* of the Lord appeared *** *(shocked reaction)* to Moses *** in flames of fire *** *(make flame shapes)* coming out of a bush *** *(make bush shape)*.

Moses *** saw *** *(saw wood)* that the bush *** was on fire *** but it was not burning up *** *(make flame shapes and say 'whoosh!')*. So *** *(sew)* Moses *** said, 'I will go closer *** *(lean forward)* to this strange thing. How can a bush *** continue burning *** *(make flame shapes)* without burning up ***?'

The Lord saw *** Moses *** coming to look *** *(hand across eyes)* at the bush ***. So *** God *** called to him from the bush ***, 'Moses ***, Moses ***'. And Moses *** said, 'Here I am, Lord ***.' Then God *** said, 'Stop *** *(hand stop sign)*! Do not come any closer *** *(wag finger)*. Take off your sandals, you are standing on holy ground.'

Moses *** covered his face *** *(cover face)* because he was afraid *** *(look frightened, biting fingernails)* to look *** at God ***. Then God *** said, 'I have seen *** *(look through binoculars)* the suffering of my people *** *(point round to audience)* and I have heard *** *(cup hand round ear)* their cries for help *** *(cry 'HELP!')*. I am concerned about their pain *** (look in pain, holding stomach). I have come down to save *** (football save!) them. I am sending you to the king *** (crown on head) of Egypt. Go *** (point to one side)! Bring my people *** out of Egypt!'

Moses was afraid *** and said, 'Who, me *** (say 'who, me?')? I'm a nobody, the king *** won't listen *** (cup hand round ear) to me!' God *** said, 'Don't worry *** (look worried, biting fingernails). I will be with you. Tell the people *** "I AM" sent you.'

But Moses *** was still worried ***. Then God *** said, 'Throw down *** (mime throwing down something) your staff.' Moses *** threw down *** his staff and it turned *** (turn round) into a snake *** (ssssss!). Quickly he ran away *** (run quickly on the spot) from it, but God *** said to him, 'Now pick the snake *** up by its tail *** (wag tail).' Moses *** obeyed God *** and the snake *** turned *** back *** (touch back) into the staff.

Next God *** told Moses *** to put his hand *** (hold up hand) inside his cloak *** (mime putting inside cloak). Moses did that and when he took it out it was covered in a terrible skin disease *** (look at hand and say 'ugh!'). Then God *** told him to put his hand *** inside his cloak *** again. This time when Moses took it out it was completely healed *** (look at hand and say 'WOW!').

'These will be two *** (show 2 fingers) signs that I AM has sent you. I AM the God *** of Abraham *** (point to the left) , Isaac *** (point to the middle) and Jacob *** (point to the right) and I will save *** my people *** from the king *** of Egypt.'

Poor Moses was still worried ***! 'But I am a very poor speaker *** (make speaking action with hand),' said Moses. God *** answered, 'Well, take your brother Aaron *** (mime 'hair on!') with you. He's a good speaker ***.'

So *** that's what happened. Moses *** and Aaron *** went to the king *** of Egypt and demanded *** (point finger) that he set God's *** people *** free *** (hands tied, then released).

MOSES IN THE BULLRUSHES

Exodus 2:1-10

Teaching point
• God is our protector

The Israelites had become slaves *** (bend over, hang head) in Egypt *** (point to the right). A lo . . . ng, long *** (say 'long' slowly and stretch out arms) time before, Joseph, Jacob his father *** (stroke beard) and all his eleven *** (count to 11 on fingers) brothers had moved from Canaan *** (point to the left) to live in Egypt *** and now there were thousands of Israelites!

One day a new king *** (crown on head) called Pharaoh *** (row a boat!) came to power in Egypt ***. He did not know about Joseph and how good *** (thumbs up) he had been to the people of Egypt ***. Pharaoh *** was worried *** (look worried, biting nails) that in time *** (look at watch) there would be so many Israelites that they would attack *** (sword fight) the people of Egypt *** and take over the land *** (mime 'over' action and aeroplane landing!). So *** (sew) Pharaoh *** ordered *** (wag finger) that the Israelites should all be made slaves ***.

Life was very hard *** (squeeze hands hard) for the Israelite slaves ***. They were whipped *** (crack a whip) and beaten *** (beat with stick) but still *** (freeze!) they increased *** (indicate growing size) in numbers. Finally, Pharaoh *** ordered *** that all the baby boys *** (suck thumb) who were under *** (duck down) two *** (show 2 fingers) years old were to be thrown *** (throwing action) into the River Nile *** (indicate river flowing) and drowned.

During this time a baby boy *** called Moses *** (mow the lawn!) was born *** (baby cry). His mother hid *** (arms over head) him in her house *** (make roof shape) away from Pharaoh's *** soldiers *** (stand to attention) but she was worried *** (look worried, biting fingernails) that when Moses *** cried *** (baby cry) the soldiers *** would hear *** (cup hand round ear) and then they would take Moses *** away and throw *** him in the River Nile ***.

So *** Moses' *** mother wrapped up her baby boy *** and put him in a basket *** (mime basket shape). She painted *** (mime painting) tar around the outside of the basket *** so that it would float *** (mime floating action) in water. Then she gave the basket *** to her daughter, Miriam, and told her to take it and put it to float *** in the bullrushes *** (run on the spot indicating horns!) on the River Nile ***.

Miriam did just that and then she hid *** to see what would happen. Shortly *** (indicate short length) after that, Pharaoh's *** daughter came down to the river *** to bathe *** (mime swimming). She spotted *** (draw spots or squeeze imaginary spot!) the basket *** in the bull-rushes *** and sent her slave girl *** to get it. She opened it and saw the baby boy ***. He was crying *** and she felt sorry *** (say 'aaah!') for him. She wanted to keep him.

Just then Miriam appeared and asked Pharaoh's *** daughter if she would like someone to nurse *** (rock baby) the baby ***. Pharaoh's daughter agreed *** (nod head) and so Miriam went home and fetched her mother to be the baby's *** nurse *** in the king's *** palace.

So *** baby *** Moses *** was saved *** (football save!) and not only that, his mother was able to see *** (look through binoculars) him and nurse *** him every day. God *** had got very big *** (indicate large shape) plans for this baby ***.

NEHEMIAH

Teaching points
- working together
- not giving up

There was once a man *** *(left, right, march on the spot)* called Nehemiah *** *(slap knee and lift it higher!)*. Nehemiah *** lived in Babylon *** *(point to the right)* but his home was in Jerusalem *** *(point to the left)*.

One day, Nehemiah *** heard *** *(cup hand round ear)* that the walls *** *(make a circle with arms)* of Jerusalem *** were broken down *** *(clap hands together crocodile-style!)*, so he asked the king *** *(crown on head)* of Babylon *** if he could go and rebuild *** *(build fist on fist)* the walls ***. The king *** of Babylon *** said he could, and promised *** *(Cubs/Brownies promise)* him all the wood *** *(knock on head)* he needed.

When Nehemiah *** reached Jerusalem *** all his friends *** *(shake hands with yourself)* met him. They were very pleased *** *(indicate big grin with index finger)* to see him, but Nehemiah *** did not tell them about his plans. He waited until it was dark and then he set off on his donkey *** *(say 'ee-aw!' or make clippety-clop noises!)* to inspect the city. The walls *** were badly broken down *** and Nehemiah *** was very sad *** *(droop head, look sad)*.

Next morning, he called the people together. 'We must build *** the walls *** again,' he said. 'God *** *(point upwards)* will help us.' Every-one agreed *** *(nod heads at one another)*. 'Let's start now,' they said. 'Let's build *** the walls *** together *** *(link arms with one another)*.' So they worked for a lo . . . ng time *(say 'long' slowly and stretch out arms)*. Some carried stones, others built *** the walls ***, some cut *** *(cut with scissors)* wood ***, others built *** the gates *** *(mime gates opening)*. Every day the walls *** grew higher *** *(stretch up)* and higher *** *(stretch up higher)*.

However, some people weren't very nice *** (say 'not nice' poshly!). They were angry *** (make an angry face) with Nehemiah *** and his men and did not want them to build *** the walls ***. They tried to stop them *** (hand signal for stop) by making fun of them *** (pull a face) and attacking them *** (pretend to fight), but the guards *** (stand to attention) drove them *** (drive car) back *** (touch back).

'You cannot frighten us *** (look terrified, biting nails). This is God's *** work and he will help us,' said Nehemiah ***. And Nehemiah *** was right *** (tick). The work went on and soon the walls *** were finished. 'God *** has helped us build *** the walls ***,' said Nehemiah ***. 'Now the city will be safe *** (hug self) and sound *** (ping!) to live in.'

They had a party *** (whoopee! party!) that lasted a whole *** (make a hole) week *** (look weak!). The priests *** (hands together, bowing head) blew *** (mime blowing out candles!) their trumpets *** (trumpet sounds) and everyone marched *** (march on the spot) along the top of the walls ***, thanking God *** and singing. They were really pleased ***, and I'm sure God *** was pleased *** also *** (all sew!).

NOAH

Genesis 6:9-8:22

Teaching points
- obedience
- following God's instructions

There once lived a man called Noah *** (*left, right, march on the spot*). Noah *** lived at a time *** (*look at watch*) when people were really wicked and evil *** (*wring hands while pulling an evil face*). They had turned *** (*turn round*) their backs (*pat back*) on God *** (*point upwards*) and were destroying *** (*thump fist on open palm*) his world *** (*indicate shape*). God *** was angry *** (*make angry expression*) about all this and decided *** (*point to side of head*) that in order to save *** (*football save*) his world *** he would have to destroy *** the whole *** (*make hole shape*) land *** (*aeroplane landing!*).

But Noah *** loved *** (*hug yourself*) God *** and always did what was right *** (*tick*). He was never wicked or evil ***. So God *** had a plan to save *** Noah ***. He said, 'Noah ***, build *** (*building action*) a lar . . . ge *** (*say 'large' slowly indicating large shape*) boat *** (*make boat shape*). Take your wife *** (*hug yourself*) and your three sons *** (*show 3 height levels*) and their wives *** (*hug yourself 3 times!*) and gather together two *** (*show 2 fingers*) of every kind of animal – sheep *** (*baa!*), pigs *** (*oink!*), cows *** (*moo!*), tigers *** (*roar!*), snakes *** (*sssss!*), birds *** (*chirp!*), monkeys *** (*chatter!*), elephants *** (*trumpet!*), frogs *** (*croak!*), dogs *** (*woof!*), cats *** (*miaow!*), and bring them all into the lar . . . ge *** boat ***. At the right time *** I will make it pour *** (*pour as from jug*) with rain *** (*show falling rain*). It will be so heavy *** (*carry heavy weight*) it will flood *** (*rising action*) the whole *** land *** and destroy *** all that is wicked and evil ***. And remember *** (*widen eyes and point*) to take plenty of food *** (*yum, yum! rub tummy*) into the boat ***.'

Noah *** did everything that God *** had commanded *** (*point as in* *giving instructions)*. The people, who were very wicked and evil ***, thought Noah *** was really silly *** *(pull a silly face)* and laughed *** *(hilarious silent laughter)* as he built the boat *** *(building action followed by boat shape)*. After all, there was no water *** *(drink glass of water noisily)* on which to sail the boat ***. But Noah *** didn't listen *** *(hands over ears)*, he trusted God ***.

When it was time *** God *** said, 'Now go into the boat *** with your whole *** family and all the animals, sheep ***, pigs ***, cows ***, tigers ***, snakes ***, birds ***, monkeys ***, elephants ***, frogs ***, dogs *** and cats ***, and I will keep you safe *** *(hug self)*.'

Then the rain *** lashed *** *(whiplash)* down, the seas *** *(look through binoculars)* flooded *** and all that was wicked and evil *** was destroyed ***. But Noah *** and his wife *** and his sons *** and their wives *** and all the animals *** *(make many animal noises!)* were kept safe *** and sound *** *(PING!)*.

PETER IN PRISON

Acts 12:1-17

Teaching points
- answer to prayer
- God's deliverance

There was once a man called Peter *** *(left, right, march on the spot)*. Peter *** was the leader *** *(salute)* of the Church *** *(make spire shape)* in Jerusalem. During that time *** *(look at watch)* there was a king *** *(indicate crown)* called Herod *** *(boo!)*. King *** Herod *** was a wicked *** *(wring hands, pulling evil face)* king ***. He had ordered *** *(wag finger with stern face)* that some of the people *** *(point round to audience)* who belonged to the Church *** should be put to death *** *(slit throat and die dramatically)*.

One day King *** Herod *** ordered *** that Peter *** should be arrested *** *(hands in handcuffs)* and thrown into prison *** *(clunk! click!)*. The people of the Church *** prayed *** *(praying hands)* to God *** *(point upwards)* to save *** *(football save)* him and set him free *** *(break out of handcuffs)*.

The night before his trial, Peter *** was sleeping *** *(head on hands and snore!)* between two *** *(show 2 fingers)* guards *** *(stand to attention x 2)*. He was in chains *** *(make chain with thumbs and forefingers)*. Suddenly *** *(gasp!)*, an angel *** *(indicate halo, saying 'ping')* of the Lord *** stood there. A light shone *** *(indicate flashing lights)* in the room and the angel *** said, 'Get dressed *** *(mime putting on clothes)* and follow me *** *(walk on spot)*'. The angel *** led Peter *** out of the prison ***. They walked *** *(walk)* past the first guard *** and the second guard *** and nobody saw *** *(saw wood)* them. They came to the gate *** *(say 'creak!' slowly)* of the prison *** – it opened *** *(opening action)* by itself. They went through the gate *** and walked *** down *** *(duck down!)* the street. Suddenly *** the angel *** left him.

Then Peter *** realised *** (look enlightened) that God *** had sent an angel *** and set him free *** from prison ***. He ran *** (run on the spot) to the house *** (make roof shape) where the believers were. They were still praying ***. He knocked *** (knock on head or furniture) on the door. A servant girl called Rhoda *** (ride a horse!) went to answer it and when she heard *** (cup hand round ear) Peter's *** voice she ran *** (run on spot) back *** (touch back) to the others and told them it was Peter ***. 'Peter *** is outside,' said Rhoda ***. 'He's knocking *** on the door.'

'You must be mad *** (act in a mad way),' they said.

Peter *** kept on knocking ***. When they finally opened *** the door and saw *** him there, they were amazed *** (look amazed, drop jaw).

He told them everything that had happened and they thanked God *** for saving *** him. Then Peter *** left Jerusalem and went to another place *** (fish swimming) where King *** Herod *** would not find him.

SAMSON

Judges 13-16

Teaching points
- bad company
- giving in to temptation

There was once a man called Samson *** *(flex arm muscles and grunt!)*. Before Samson *** was born *** *(baby cry)*, the angel *** *(indicate halo)* of the Lord *** *(point upwards)* had appeared to his mother and had told her that Samson *** was going to be a very special baby *** *(rock baby)*. The angel *** of the Lord *** also said that Samson *** was never *** *(shake head warningly, wag finger)* to have his hair *** *(brush hair)* cut *** *(cut with scissors)*, and that one day God *** would use him to save *** *(football save)* his people, the Israelites, from the Philistines *** *(boo!)*. When Samson *** was born *** God *** made him very strong *** *(flex muscles)*.

One day, Samson *** and his father and mother were on a journey when suddenly *** *(sudden, shocked reaction)* a lion *** *(ROAR!)* sprang out *** *(pounce or spring up!)* and came roaring *** *(ROAR!)* towards them. God *** gave Samson *** great strength *** and power *** *(punch fist, POW!)*. He tore *** *(tear paper)* the lion *** apart with his bare hands *** *(show hands, palms forward)*.

Another time *** *(look at watch)* God *** gave Samson *** so much strength *** and power *** that he killed *** *(slit throat!)* 1,000 *** *(show 1 finger and 3 noughts)* Philistines ***. Samson *** was the leader *** *(salute)* of the people of Israel for 20 years *** *(show 10 fingers twice)*.

However, one day, Samson *** fell in love *** *(aah!)* with a woman called Delilah *** *(say 'oh, no!')*. Delilah was bad news *** *(towncrier 'Oyez! Oyez!')*. She was really wicked and evil *** *(wring hands, pull evil face)* and the leaders *** of the Philistines *** went to her and promised to give her money *** (stroke palm) if she would find out the secret *** (shh!) of Samson's *** strength *** and power ***.

Delilah *** agreed and over and over again *** (rolling action with forearms) she tried to make Samson *** tell her his secret ***. Sadly, *** (cry dramatically) one day he gave in and told Delilah *** that if his hair *** was cut *** then he would lose all his strength *** and power ***.

That night Delilah *** cut *** off Samson's *** hair *** while he was asleep *** (head on hands) and then when Samson *** was powerless *** (flop!) the Philistine *** soldiers *** (stand to attention) arrested him, took out his eyes *** (ugh!) and threw him into prison *** (CLUNK! Shut door, CLICK! Turn key).

Sometime *** later, the Philistines *** were having a party *** (party!) to celebrate the capture *** (hug self) of Samson ***, and they brought him out to laugh at him *** (laugh mockingly). Samson *** was blind *** (cover eyes) and he asked to be put between two large pillars *** (head on pillow and snore!). He cried out to God *** for help *** (shout 'HELP!') and then he pushed *** (push) against the pillars ***. God gave Samson *** strength *** and power *** again. The pillars *** fell down and all the building collapsed *** (clap hands crocodile-style!).

And although Samson *** died *** (die dramatically) that day, so did many Philistines *** and it was a great victory for the people of Israel. HOORAY (all cheer)!

SAMUEL

1 Samuel 1, 3

Teaching points
- obedience
- hearing God's voice

A very long *** *(say 'long' slowly, stretching out arms)* time ago *** *(look at watch)* there lived a woman called Hannah. Hannah was very sad *** *(cry dramatically!)* because she longed *** to have a baby *** *(suck thumb)*. One year when she went to God's holy tent *** *(tent shape)* in Shiloh *** *(look shy and bend low!)* she prayed to God *** *(praying hands, point upwards)* that she would have a baby ***. She promised *** *(Cub/Brownie salute, point upwards)* that if he gave her a son, she would give the boy back *** *(indicate short person and touch back)* to God *** so that he could serve him *** *(tennis serve)*.

When Eli the priest *** *(bow, hands together)* saw Hannah *** *(sawing action)*, he thought she was drunk *** *(sway about, 'hic!')* because she was praying in her heart *** *(hands together, hand on heart)*, her lips were moving *** *(move lips)*, but her voice was not heard *** *(silent, mouthed 'voice')*. Hannah explained to Eli the priest *** that she was not drunk ***, but was asking God *** for a baby son ***. 'Go in peace,' said Eli the priest ***, 'and may God *** give you what you asked of him.'

God heard Hannah's prayer *** and some time later *** *(circle watch)*, Samuel was born *** *(baby cry)*. Hannah kept her promise *** and when he was old enough she took Samuel to Eli the priest *** in Shiloh *** and presented him to the Lord *** so that he might serve *** God in his holy tent ***.

Samuel grew to love God *** *(indicate growth, hug self, point upwards)*, and he helped Eli the priest ***. One night Samuel heard a voice call his name *** *(whisper 'Samuel')*. He thought it was Eli the priest ***, so he went to see *** (indicate binoculars) what he wanted. 'I did not call you,' he said. 'Go back to bed *** (touch back, head on hands).'

So *** (sew) Samuel went back to bed ***. This happened a second time *** (show 2 fingers, circle watch) and a third time *** (show 3 fingers, circle watch). Then Eli the priest *** realised that it must be God *** calling Samuel's name ***. He told Samuel to go back to bed *** and if God *** called his name again *** he was to say, 'Here I am, Lord *** (say 'Here I am, Lord')'.

And that is exactly what happened. God told Samuel to give Eli the priest *** a very hard message *** (squeeze hands together, showing effort). God said that because Eli's sons were so wicked and evil *** (wring hands, pull face) they would be killed *** (stab chest) and Eli would die too *** (die dramatically!), because he had not corrected his sons, nor had he stopped *** (stop sign) them doing wicked and evil things ***. Also *** (all sew), God said that none of his family would be priests *** in Shiloh ***.

Samuel was afraid *** (tremble, bite fingernails) to tell Eli the priest *** God's message, but Eli asked him what God *** had said. When Eli heard the message he knew that it was right *** (tick) and that it was fair. He was not cross *** (draw X) with Samuel for telling him this.

All that God *** said about Eli the priest *** and his family came to pass but Samuel grew up *** (indicate growth, point upwards) to be God's leader in Israel *** (point upwards, salute).

SHADRACH, MESHACH AND ABEDNEGO

Daniel 3

Teaching point
• worship only God

King Nebuchadnezzar *** *(crown on head)* was the ruler *** *(indicate shape of a ruler!)* of Babylon. He was a very powerful *** *(flex muscles)* king *** and he was also a very proud *** *(lift head with finger under nose!)* king ***. He thought that he was the most important *** *(look important, holding lapels)* person in the world *** *(make world shape)*.

One day he decided that a statue *** *(be a statue)* should be built *** *(building action)* and that all the people *** *(point round to audience)* should bow down *** *(bow head slowly)* and worship *** *(full bowing down action)* it. The statue *** was massive *** *(indicate very large shape)*. It was 90 *** *(show 9 x 10 fingers)* feet *** *(hold nose, say 'pooh!')* high *** *(indicate height)* and nine *** *(show 9 fingers)* feet *** wide *** *(indicate width)*.

King Nebuchadnezzar *** ordered *** *(wag finger)* that whenever the music played *** *(conduct)* with the sound of the horn *** *(blow horn or indicate animal horns!)*, the flute *** *(blow flute sideways)*, the zither *** *(horizontal instrument to be plucked)*, the lyre *** *(play as a guitar)* and the harp *** *(pluck harp)*, everyone had to bow down *** and worship *** the statue ***. If any of the people *** refused to bow down *** they were to be thrown *** *(mime throwing action)* into a fiery furnace *** *(indicate flames)*.

Now many of God's *** *(point upwards)* people lived in the land of Babylon. King Nebuchadnezzar *** had taken them prisoner *** *(hands tied at wrists)* many years before *** *(show 4 fingers!)*. Shadrach *** *(point to the left)*, Meshach *** *(point to the centre)* and Abednego *** *(point to the right)* were three *** *(show 3 fingers)* of those prisoners ***.

Shadrach ***, Meshach *** and Abednego *** loved God *** and they knew it was wrong to bow down *** and worship *** the statue ***. So *** (sew) when the music played ***, Shadrach ***, Meshach *** and Abednego *** did not bow down *** and worship *** the statue ***.

Now some of the people *** did not like *** (turn up nose and say 'ugh') Shadrach, *** Meshach *** and Abednego *** and they went and told King Nebuchadnezzar *** that these three *** men would not bow down *** and worship *** the statue *** when they heard the horn ***, the flute ***, the zither ***, the lyre *** and the harp ***.

The king *** was furious *** (stamp feet, be really angry) when he heard *** (cup hand round ear) and commanded *** (wag finger) that Shadrach ***, Meshach *** and Abednego *** should be brought before him. 'Is it true?' he said. 'Will you not bow down *** and worship *** the golden statue ***?'

'No,' said the three *** men, 'we will only worship the one *** (show 1 finger) true *** (hands crossed over heart) God ***.'

King Nebuchadnezzar *** was even more furious *** and ordered *** that the fiery furnace *** should be heated up seven *** (show 7 fingers) times hotter. It was so hot that the guards *** (stand to attention) who took Shadrach ***, Meshach *** and Abednego *** away and threw *** them into the fiery furnace *** were killed *** (die dramatically) immediately by the flames ***.

The king watched *** (look at watch!) as the men fell into the fiery furnace ***. But what was this? Shadrach ***, Meshach *** and Abednego *** were not being burned and now there were four *** (show 4 fingers) men walking *** (walk on the spot) about in the flames ***. The fourth *** man was the angel *** (indicate halo) of God ***.

King Nebuchadnezzar *** went nearer the fiery furnace *** and told the men to come out. So *** Shadrach ***, Meshach *** and Abednego *** came out. None of their clothes *** (pull own clothes) were burnt nor did they smell of smoke *** (sniff a few times). God *** had saved them from the fire ***.

After that, King Nebuchadnezzar *** commanded *** that no one was to say anything against the God *** of Shadrach ***, Meshach *** and Abednego ***, because he was the most powerful *** of all gods – the only one *** true *** God ***.

THE CONVERSION OF SAUL

Acts 9:1-22

Teaching point
• salvation

One day, a man called Saul *** *(left, right, march on the spot)* set off on his donkey *** *(ee-aw!)*. He was travelling from Jerusalem *** *(point to the right)* to Damascus *** *(point to the left)* to arrest all the followers *** *(walk on spot)* of Jesus *** *(point upwards or use deaf signing action, i.e. touch nail prints in palm of each hand with opposite middle finger)*.

The sun was shining *** *(indicate sun rays)*, the sky was blue *** *(blow)* as the donkey *** trotted along the road. Saul *** and his men had travelled a long *** *(say 'long' slowly, stretching out arms)* time *** *(look at watch)*. They were hot *** *(say 'phew!' wiping hand across forehead)* and tired *** *(drop head and go limp)*.

Suddenly *** *(shocked reaction, gasp)*, when they got near to the city of Damascus ***, a bright light shone *** *(indicate bright light)* all around them *** *(turn full circle)*. Saul *** fell to the ground and heard a voice *** *(say 'voice!' strongly)* saying to him, 'Saul ***, Saul ***, why are you persecuting me *** *(hit chest with fist)*?'

'Who are you, Lord *** *(point upwards)*?' said Saul.

'I am Jesus ***, whom you are persecuting ***,' said the voice ***. 'But get up *** *(indicate rising action)*, and go into Damascus *** where you will be told *** *(wag finger)* what to do.'

The men who were travelling with Saul *** and the donkey *** had stopped *** *(stop hand signal)*. They had heard *** *(cup hand round ear)* the voice *** but could not see *** *(look through binoculars)* anything. Saul *** got up ***, opened his eyes *** *(open eyes wide)* but could not see *** a thing. So *** *(sew)* the men took him by the hand *** *(hold up hand)* and led him into Damascus ***.

Now in Damascus *** there lived a follower *** of Jesus *** called Ananias, and God *** *(point upwards)* told *** him to go to a street called Straight Street *** *(stand straight)* where he would find Saul ***. At first Ananias was afraid *(look afraid, biting nails)* to go because he had heard *** how Saul *** had been persecuting *** the followers *** of Jesus ***. But finally he agreed *** *(nod head several times)* to go to Straight Street *** and he laid his hands *** *(show hands)* on Saul ***. He said, 'Brother Saul ***, the Lord *** has sent me so *** that you can see *** again and be filled with the Holy Spirit'.

At once something like fish *** *(fish swimming)* scales *** *(move hands in balancing motion)* fell from Saul's *** eyes *** and he was able to see ***. He got up and was baptised *** *(mime baptism)*.

From that time *** Saul *** changed. He began to tell all the people *** *(point round the audience)* that Jesus *** was God's *** Son, and all the followers *** were amazed *(look amazed, drop jaw, say 'WOW!')*.

NB: A donkey is not referred to in the Bible passage!

THE FEEDING OF THE FIVE THOUSAND

Matthew 14:13-21; Mark 6:32-44;
Luke 9:10-17; John 6:1-13

Teaching points
- Jesus can work miracles
- God's provision

One day Jesus *** (*use deaf signing action, i.e. touch nail prints in palm of each hand with opposite middle finger*) went out onto the hillside *** (*indicate hill and the side of body*) and a large crowd of people *** (*indicate a large semicircle in front of you*) followed *** (*walk on the spot*) him. Soon there were about five *** (*show 5 fingers*) thousand men *** (*indicate tall height*) not including women *** (*indicate a lower height*) and children *** (*indicate short height*).

All day Jesus *** talked *** (*mime speaking with hand*) to the people ***, telling them about God *** (*point upwards*) and how they should live. After a long *** (*say 'long' slowly and stretch out arms*) time *** (*look at watch*) the disciples *** (*show 12 fingers*) said to Jesus ***, 'It's getting late, send the people away *** (*point to one side*) so that they can buy *** (*wave 'bye'*) food *** (*rub tummy*) from the surrounding *** (*draw circle in front of you horizontally*) villages.'

Jesus *** said, 'You give them something to eat *** (*mime eating*).'

They said to him, 'But we have no money *** (*rub palm of hand or mime empty pockets*) and anyway there's nowhere round here *** (*turn round*) to buy *** food ***.'

Jesus *** said, 'Go *** (*point forward*) and see *** (*look through binoculars*) what food *** there is.'

The disciples *** soon found a small boy *** (*indicate short height*) who had five *** loaves and two *** (*show 2 fingers*) fish *** (*mime fish *swimming)*. The small boy *** was pleased *** *(indicate smiley face)* to give his five *** loaves and two *** fish *** to Jesus ***.

Then Jesus *** told the disciples *** to tell all the people *** to sit down *** *(mime sitting down)* in groups of one hundred *** *(show 10 x 10 fingers)* or fifty *** *(show 5 x10 fingers)*. Jesus *** took the five *** loaves and two *** fish ***, looked up to heaven *** *(look upwards)*, and gave thanks to God ***. He broke *** *(mime breaking)* the bread and fish *** and gave it to the disciples *** to give it out *** *(mime sharing out)* to the people ***.

They all ate *** the food *** and were full up *** *(mime being full)*. The disciples *** picked up twelve *** baskets *** *(make circle with arms)* full *** of broken *** pieces of bread and fish ***. Jesus *** had done a miracle *** *(say 'WOW!')*. He had fed five *** thousand men *** and women *** and children *** with only five *** loaves and two *** fish ***. WOW!

THE GOOD SAMARITAN

Luke 10:25-37

Teaching point
• love your neighbour

One day a teacher of the law *** (wag finger) asked Jesus *** (point upwards or use deaf signing action, i.e. touch nail prints of each hand with opposite middle finger) a question *** (mime a question mark). He said, 'Who is my neighbour *** (neigh!)?' To answer this, Jesus *** told this story *** (open book as in charades).

'There was once a man *** (left, right, march on the spot) who was travelling from Jerusalem *** (point to the right) to Jericho *** (point to the left). On the way he was attacked *** (mime fighting) by robbers *** (mime using a rubber – leader says 'robbers' not 'rubbers'!). They kicked him *** (kick) and beat him *** (beat as with stick) and tore off his clothes *** (mime tearing off clothes). They stole *** (grabbing action) all his money *** (show empty pockets) and left him for dead *** (die dramatically!).

'Not long *** (say 'long' slowly, stretching out arms) after, a Jewish priest *** (hands together, bowing head) was passing by. When the priest *** saw *** (saw wood) the man *** he walked by *** (walk on spot) on the other side *** (indicate side of body) of the road *** (indicate bend shape).

'Next, a Levite came along. Now Levites were men *** (left, right, march on the spot x 2) from the tribe of Levi *** (make some comment about jeans, e.g. 'Mmm . . . 501s?' – leader corrects) who helped the Jewish priests *** (hands together, bowing head x 2) in the temple *** (make spire shape). The Levite went over *** (mime the word 'over') and looked *** (hand across eyes) at the man ***. Then he too *** (show 2 fingers) walked by *** on the other side *** of the road ***. Perhaps he was afraid *** (look fearful, biting nails) that the robbers *** would attack *** him also *** (all sew).

'Shortly after *** (indicate short length) a Samaritan *** (ugh!) came along. He saw *** the man *** lying almost dead *** by the roadside *** (mime bend in road and touch side). He felt very sorry *** (cry dramatically) for him and poured *** (pour) olive oil *** (say 'oh, Popeye!') and wine *** (hic!) on his wounds and bandaged them *** (mime bandaging a wound). Then the Samaritan *** put the hurt man *** on his donkey *** (ee-aw!) and took him to an inn *** (sing 'In out, in out, shake it all about!')

'There the Samaritan *** looked after *** (look forward with hand across eyes) him. The next day he gave the inn *** keeper two *** (show 2 fingers) silver coins *** (make 2 small coin shapes) and said, "Look after *** this man *** and if you spend more money *** (stroke palm of hand) on him, I will pay it back to you *** (touch back and point to audience!) when I come again."'

Then Jesus *** said, 'Which one of these three men *** (left, right, march on the spot x 3) do you think *** (finger to side of head) was a neighbour *** to the man *** who was attacked *** by robbers ***?'

The teacher of the law *** answered, 'The Samaritan ***, the one who helped'.

Jesus *** said to him, 'Then go *** (point forward) and do the same thing.'

THE HOUSE ON THE ROCK

Matthew 7:24-27; Luke 6:47-49

Teaching points
- obeying Jesus' instructions
- building our lives on Jesus

There was once a man *** (*left, right, march on the spot*), who decided to build a house *** (*make roof shape*). So he looked around *** (*look through binoculars and turn round*) for a suitable place to build his house ***.

It wasn't lo . . . ng *** (*say 'long' slowly, moving hands outward as in measuring*), before he found just the right spot *** (*point to an exact spot or pretend to squeeze a spot!*). What an incredible view *** (*peer forward with hand across eyes*)! What amazing hills *** (*make hill shape*) and streams *** (*make running water action*)! What gorgeous trees *** (*make unusual tree shape*)! Oh, and the lake *** (*WOW!*)! So he began to build his new house *** near the lake ***, on the sand *** (*oh, no!*).

Meanwhile there was another man *** who had decided to build a house ***. So he looked around *** for a suitable place to build his house ***. It took him a lo . . . ng time *** (*say 'long' even slower and look at watch*) to find just the right spot ***. It had to be hard *** (*stamp right foot*), it had to be firm *** (*stamp left foot*), and it had to be flat *** (*indicate flat surface*). He didn't mind so much about the view ***, as long as he would be safe *** (*hug yourself*) and sound *** (*ping!*) inside the house ***. So *** he began to build his house *** on a strong *** (*flex arm muscles*), firm ***, flat *** rock *** (*fist*).

After several weeks the two men *** (*left, right, march on the spot x 2*), had finished their houses *** (*make roof shapes x 2*), and they began to look forward *** (*lean forward with hand across eyes*) to a lo . . . ng *** life in their new houses ***.

However, shortly after they had moved in, there was a terrible storm. The rain lashed down *** (whiplash), the wind roared *** (ROAR!) around the houses ***. But the house *** built on the strong ***, hard ***, flat *** rock *** stood firm *** (fist on fist). Hooray *** (all cheer)!

But sad to say *** (boo-hoo!), the house *** built on the sand *** began to wobble *** (wobble) and shake *** (shake) and rock from side to side *** (rock), and as the wind roared *** and the rain lashed down ***, the house *** on the sand *** fell down *** (fall down or clap hands crocodile-style!). And that was that – FLAT *** (lie flat or clap hands and say FLAT)!

THE LAME MAN

Acts 3:1-10

Teaching point
- healing
- power of God

There was once a lame man *** *(go weak at the knees!)*. Every day he sat begging *** *(beg like a dog!)* at the Beautiful Gate *** *(WOW!)* of the temple *** *(make steeple shape)*. Not long *** *(say 'long' slowly, stretching out arms)* after Pentecost when the Holy Spirit came *** *(make sound of wind and flame shapes)*, Peter *** *(lightly stamp one foot)* and John *** *(lightly stamp the other)* were on their way to the temple *** to praise God *** *(shout 'hallelujah', raising hands)*. They had to pass through the Beautiful Gate *** where the lame man *** was begging ***.

'Please *** *(pleading)* sirs, can you spare some money *** *(stroke palm of hand)*?' said the lame man ***. Peter *** and John *** stopped *** *(make stop sign)* and said to him, 'We don't have any money *** *(show empty pockets)*, but what we do have, we will give to you. In the name of Jesus Christ *** *(use deaf signing action, i.e. touch nail prints in palm of each hand with opposite middle finger)* of Nazareth, get up and walk *** *(rising up action and walk on spot)*.'

Then Peter *** took the lame man *** by the right hand *** *(hold out right hand)* and pulled him up *** *(pulling up action)*. Immediately, the lame man's *** feet and ankles *** *(hold nose! pooh!)* became strong *** *(flex muscles)*. He jumped *** *(big jump)* to his feet *** and began to walk *** *(walk on spot)*. He followed Peter *** and John *** into the temple ***. He was walking *** and leaping *** *(bounce up and down)* and praising God *** *(raise hands, shouting 'hallelujah!' x 3)*.

When the people saw *** *(saw wood!)* the lame man *** walking *** and leaping *** and praising God *** they were amazed *** *(look surprised)*! 'This man is over 40 years old *** *(indicate 4 x 10 fingers)*,' they thought. 'He's been begging *** at the Beautiful Gate *** every day for as long as we can remember *** *(point to side of head, thinking)*'.

Peter *** and John *** were quick to tell them that it was Jesus *** who had healed the lame man ***. It was his power *** *(explosion!)* not their own. Since the Holy Spirit came at Pentecost *** Peter *** and John *** and all the disciples were filled with God's power ***.

And so *** *(sew)* the lame man *** was now a strong man ***, and he went on his way walking *** and leaping *** and praising God ***!

THE LOST SHEEP

Matthew 18:12-14; Luke 15:4-7

Teaching points
- God loves each one of us
- God seeks the lost

There was once a man *** (*left, right, march on the spot*). This man *** owned 100 *** (*show 10 fingers 10 times*) sheep *** (*baa!*). These sheep *** used to graze *** (*munch*) on the hillside *** (*indicate hill, touch side*) while the man *** kept watch *** (*look at watch*).

One day the man *** was counting *** (*count*) his sheep *** when he discovered that there were only 99 *** (*show 10 fingers 9 times and then 9*) sheep ***. The man *** was shocked *** (*look suitably shocked, drop jaw!*), and stunned *** (*hand over open mouth!*) and very surprised *** (*mouth open, hands on head*). He began to count *** the sheep *** again, yet still he only saw *** (*saw wood*) 99 *** sheep ***. One *** (*show 1 finger*) sheep *** was definitely missing.

So *** (*sew*) the man *** left the 99 *** sheep *** grazing *** on the hillside *** and he went to see *** (*mime sea or looking through binoculars*) if he could find the lost sheep ***. The man *** looked high *** (*stretch up*) and low *** (*crouch down*) for the sheep *** when suddenly *** (*sudden, shocked reaction*) he heard *** (*cup hand round ear*) a faint noise *** (*whisper 'noise'!*). And to his surprise *** (*eyes wide, drop jaw*) he saw *** his lost sheep ***.

The man *** was very happy *** (*hilarious silent laughter*) and he picked up the sheep *** and put it on his shoulders *** (*touch shoulders*). He carried his sheep *** home. The man *** was so happy *** he threw *** (*pretend to throw something*) a big *** (*indicate something large*) party *** (*party!*) and he invited all his friends *** (*shake your own hands*) and neighbours *** (*neigh!*).

The man *** cared for his sheep *** so much that even if only one *** sheep *** went missing, he would go and look *** for it and bring it back *** *(touch back)*. And that's just how God *** *(point upwards)* cares for you *** *(point to everyone)* and me *** *(point to self)*.

THE PARALYSED MAN

Matthew 9:2-8; Mark 2:3-12; Luke 5:18-26

Teaching points
- the healing power of Jesus
- forgiveness of sins
- faithfulness of friends

There was once a man who couldn't walk *** *(walk on the spot)*, who couldn't run *** *(run on the spot)*, who couldn't jump *** *(jump on the spot)* and who certainly couldn't dance *** *(dance on the spot)*! He was paralysed *** *(go weak at the knees)* and all day long *** *(say 'long' slowly and stretch out arms)* he lay on his bed, unable to do anything.

But this paralysed *** man, who couldn't walk *** or run *** or jump *** and certainly couldn't dance ***, had four *** *(show 4 fingers)* very good *** *(thumbs up)* friends *** *(shake hands with self)* and one day they heard *** *(cup hand round ear)* some very good *** news. Jesus *** *(point upwards or use deaf signing action, i.e. touch nail prints in palm of each hand with opposite middle finger)* was in a house *** *(indicate a house shape)* nearby.

They quickly carried their friend ***, who couldn't walk *** or run *** or jump *** and certainly couldn't dance ***, to the house ***, but when they got there, there were crowds of people *** *(indicate large group of people)*. They couldn't get anywhere near the door *** *(mime opening door)*. Then they had an idea *** *(eyes light up, point to side of head)*. They carried the paralysed *** man up the steps *** *(mime ascending steps)* onto the flat roof *** *(indicate flat roof)*.

Soon they were making a hole *** *(make a hole shape with arms)* in the flat roof ***. Then they carefully lowered *** *(go lower)* their friend *** down to where Jesus *** was standing. Jesus *** looked up *** *(look up)* and saw *** *(saw wood)* the four *** friends ***. He knew that they really believed he would heal their paralysed *** friend ***. So *** *(sew)* he did! Not only that. Jesus also *** *(all sew!)* forgave the man's sins.

The four *** friends *** were really pleased *** *(indicate smiley face)* but not nearly so excited *** *(be excited!)* as the paralysed *** man, because now he could walk *** and run *** and jump *** and yes, he certainly could dance ***!

THE PHARISEE AND THE TAX-COLLECTOR

Luke 18:9-14

Teaching points
- how to pray
- humility
- forgiveness

There was once a man *** *(left, right, march on the spot)*, who went to church *** *(make spire shape or point to everyone)* to pray *** *(hands together)*. This man thought *** *(point to side of head)* that he was great *** *(thumbs up)*. He thought *** he was clever *** *(breathe on knuckles and rub on chest)*. He even thought *** he was a saint *** *(indicate halo and say 'ping!')*. So *** *(sew)* when he went to church *** to pray ***, he wanted everyone to see him *** *(look through binoculars)*, and hear him *** *(cup hand round ear)*, and admire him *** *(throw hands back and say 'aah!')*.

So *** this man *** stood where everyone could see him *** and he prayed *** to God *** in a very loud voice *** *(shout 'VOICE!')*, so everyone could hear ***. And he told God *** how great *** he was, how clever *** he was and how he really was a saint ***. And the people all admired him *** and he thought *** he was all right *** *(tick!)* with God *** and that God *** admired him *** too. But he didn't *** *(shake head)*!

Now there was another man *** who also went to church *** to pray ***. This man *** knew he wasn't great ***, he knew he wasn't clever ***, and he certainly knew he wasn't a saint ***. He knew he wasn't right *** with God ***. He felt ashamed *** *(lower head)* and sorry *** *(cry dramatically)*. He didn't want anyone to see him *** or hear him ***. So *** this man *** stood at a distance and prayed *** honestly, in a very quiet voice *** *(whisper 'voice!')*, 'Please, God ***, I'm sorry ***.' He thought *** God *** would dislike him *** *(unpleasant expression and* *say 'yuk!')*. But he didn't ***! In fact, it was the second man ***, the honest man ***, the humble man *** who went home right *** with God ***. And that was all right ***!

THE SHEPHERDS

Luke 2:8-20

Teaching point
• to tell the Christmas story

There were shepherds *** (ooh argh!) living out in the fields near Bethlehem *** (point to one side), keeping watch *** (look at watch) over their sheep *** (baa!). Suddenly *** (sudden, shocked reaction), an angel *** (indicate halo) of the Lord *** (point upwards) appeared. The shepherds *** were terrified *** (look terrified, biting nails). The angel *** said, 'Do not be terrified ***, I bring you good news *** (towncrier 'OYEZ! OYEZ!') which will be for all people *** (point to everyone). Today in Bethlehem *** a baby *** (rock baby in arms) has been born, who will save *** (football save) people *** (point to everyone). He is Christ the Lord ***. This will be a sign to you. You will find the baby *** wrapped in cloths and lying in a manger *** (hold nose and say 'pooh!').

Suddenly *** lots of angels *** (indicate several halos) appeared with the angel ***, praising God *** and saying, 'Glory to God *** in the highest and on earth peace to all people *** with whom he is pleased *** (indicate smiley face).' The shepherds *** were amazed *** (look amazed and say 'WOW!').

When the angels *** had left them and gone back *** (touch back) into heaven the shepherds *** said to one another, 'Let's leave our sheep *** and go to Bethlehem *** and see *** (look through binoculars) this thing that has happened which the Lord *** has told us about'.

So *** (sew) the shepherds *** hurried off to Bethlehem ***. There they found Mary and Joseph and Jesus, the baby *** who was lying in a manger ***. When the shepherds *** had seen the baby *** they spread

the news *** about what the angel *** had said to them about the baby
***. The people *** who heard it *** *(cup hand round ear)* were amazed
*** at the good news *** the shepherds *** had told them. The shepherds *** went back *** praising God *** for what they had seen ***
and heard ***. They had seen *** the baby *** in the manger *** just
as they had been told by the angel ***. Wasn't that amazing ***!

THE STILLING OF THE STORM

Matthew 8:23-27; Mark 4:36-41; Luke 8:22-25

Teaching points
- trust
- Jesus has power over nature

One day, Jesus *** (point upwards or use deaf signing, i.e. touch nail prints in palm of each hand with opposite middle finger) and his followers *** (walk on the spot) climbed *** (mime climbing a ladder) into a boat (rowing action) and went across *** (look cross-eyed!) to the other side *** (touch side) of the lake *** (indicate water). Shortly *** (indicate short person or length) after they had set sail *** (hoist up sail), Jesus *** fell *** (mime tripping over) asleep *** (head on hands and snore) in the back *** (touch back) of the boat ***.

Before they had got across ***, a very strong *** (flex muscles) wind *** (blow strongly) blew up *** (explosion!) on the lake ***. The waves *** (mime waves) came up *** (pretend to vomit!) over the boat *** and soon the boat *** was filled with water *** (slurp, slurp!)

All this time *** (look at watch), Jesus *** was in the back *** of the boat *** fast *** (run on the spot) asleep ***. His followers were terrified *** (look terrified, biting nails) and panicked *** (panic!). They went to Jesus *** and when they saw *** (saw wood) that he was still fast *** asleep ***, they woke him up *** (mime shaking someone). They shouted, 'Master, Master, we will drown *** (shout 'Master, Master, we will drown!')!

Jesus *** woke up *** (mime waking up suddenly) and spoke to the wind *** and the waves ***. Immediately, the wind *** stopped *** (stop sign) blowing *** (blow), the waves *** no longer came up *** over the boat *** and the lake *** became calm *** (spread hands flat).

Then Jesus *** said to his followers ***, 'Why were you afraid ***? Where is your faith?'

The followers *** were afraid *** and amazed *** *(look amazed, drop jaw)*. They said to each other, 'What kind of man is this? Even the wind *** and the waves *** obey him!'

THE TWO SONS

Luke 15:11-32

Teaching point
- God's love and forgiveness

There was once *** *(show 1 finger)* a man who had two sons *** *(left, right, march on the spot)*. The younger son *** *(stamp left foot lightly on the spot)* was fed up *** *(look fed up)* at home *** *(make roof shape)*. He dreamed *** *(close eyes, head on hands and snore!)* of an exciting life far away *** *(look forward, hand across eyes)*.

One day he decided to leave home ***, so *** *(sew)* he went to his dad and said, 'Dad, I know that part of your land *** *(aeroplane landing)* is mine. I want you to give me the money *** *(rub palm)* now for my share of the land ***.'

So *** the father gave his son *** *(indicate short height)* the money *** he wanted. The son *** took it all and went far away ***. At first he was very happy *** *(hilarious silent laughter)* doing whatever he wanted to do. He went wherever he wanted to go, and used the money *** to buy *** *(wave 'bye'!)* whatever he wanted.

Before long *** *(say 'long' slowly and stretch out arms)* he had spent all his money ***, and he did not have even enough to buy *** food *** *(yum, yum! rub tummy)*. A severe famine *** *(hold stomach and look really hungry)* spread *** *(mime spreading bread and butter!)* over *** *(mime 'arm over')* the land ***.

So *** he got a job feeding the pigs *** *(oink!)*. He longed *** to eat *** *(mime eating)* the food *** that he was giving to the pigs ***, because no one gave him anything to eat ***.

At last he came to his senses and thought *** (point to side of head) to himself, 'All my father's workers *** (sing 'Hi Ho! Hi Ho! It's off to work we go') back at home *** have more food *** than they can eat ***, yet here I am starving to death *** (hold stomach and die dramatically). I will get up *** (get up!) and go back home *** (touch back and make roof shape) to my father and say, "I have sinned against heaven *** (point upwards) and against you *** (point to audience) and I don't deserve to be your son ***. Treat me like one of your workers ***."' So *** he got up *** and set off back home ***.

While he was still far away *** his father saw *** (saw wood) him coming. He ran *** (run on the spot) out to meet him, threw his arms around him *** (hug self) and kissed *** (mime two kisses) him. Before the son *** could say very much, his father said, 'Let's have a party *** (party!).' He said to his servants, 'Bring the best robe *** (hold lapels) and put it on him, put a ring *** (indicate ring on finger) on his finger and shoes on his feet *** (hold nose, saying 'pooh!'). Then go and get the prize calf *** (moo!) and kill it *** (stab chest). We are going to have a party *** because this son *** of mine was dead *** and is alive again, he was lost and is found.'

So *** that is what they did. They had one big, splendid party *** – with lots of lovely food ***. The younger son *** was certainly happy *** to be back home *** with his father, and surprised that even though he had wasted all his money *** his father had still welcomed him back home ***.

(This last paragraph may be omitted)

[But sad to say *** (boo-hoo!) the older son *** (stamp right foot lightly on the spot) was not at all pleased ***. He was grumpy *** (look grumpy) and jealous *** (narrow eyes, glare) and angry *** (look angry, raise a fist) with his father because he had done this.]

THE UNFORGIVING SERVANT

Matthew 18:21-35

Teaching points
- God's forgiveness
- our forgiveness

Peter *** *(left, right, march on the spot)* once said to Jesus *** *(use deaf signing action, i.e. touch nail prints in palm of each hand with opposite middle finger)*, 'Lord *** *(point upwards)*, how many times *** *(make X with index fingers)* shall I forgive *** *(show 4 fingers then give offering)* my brother when he sins against me *** *(point to self)*? Up *** *(look up)* to seven *** *(show 7 fingers)* times ***?' Jesus answered, 'I tell you, not seven *** times ***, but 77 *** *(show 7 x 10 and 7 fingers)* times ***.' So *** *(sew)* Jesus *** told this story *** *(open book as in charades)*.

'There was once a king *** *(crown on head)* who wanted to collect in the money *** *(stroke palm)* his servants *** *(bow head with hands together several times)* owed him. As the king *** began, a servant *** *(bow head with hands together once)* who owed him 10,000 talents *** *(start counting up to 10,000 in 10s really fast and then give up!)* (that was several million pounds), was brought before the king ***. Since he was not able to pay *** *(mime paying out money)*, the king *** ordered that the servant ***, his wife *** *(mime two kisses or skirt movement!)* and his children *** *(indicate descending heights)* and all that he had, was to be sold *** *(point to bottom of shoe!)* to repay the debt.

'The servant *** fell *** *(mime chopping tree down and shout 'Timber!')* to his knees *** *(point to knees)* before him. "Please be patient *** *(say 'Doctor, I feel really sick!')* with me," the man begged *** *(beg like a dog)*, "and I will pay *** you everything."

'The king *** took pity *** *(say 'aaahh!')* on the servant *** and cancelled *** *(make an X)* the debt and let him go.

'When the servant *** went out he found one *** *(show 1 finger)* of his fellow servants ***, who owed him 100 *** *(show 10 x 10 fingers)* denarii (that was just a few pounds). The first servant *** grabbed *** *(grab by collar)* him and began to choke *** *(mime choking)* him. "Pay back *** *(pay out money and touch back)* what you owe me!" the servant *** demanded. His fellow servant *** fell *** to his knees *** and begged *** him, "Please be patient *** with me and I will pay *** you everything." But the servant *** refused and had the man *** thrown into prison *** *(mime and say 'clunk! click!')* until he could pay *** the debt.

'When the other servants *** saw *** *(saw wood)* what had happened, they were greatly distressed *** *(cry dramatically)* and went and told the king *** everything that had happened.

'So *** *(sew)* the king *** called his servant *** in. "You wicked *** *(wring hands, pulling an evil face)* servant ***," said the king ***. "I have cancelled *** all that debt of yours because you begged *** me to. Shouldn't you have had mercy on your fellow servant ***?"

'In anger *** *(look angry)* the king *** turned him over *** *(turn around and mime 'over')* to the jailers until his debt was paid in full.'

'So ***,' said Jesus ***, 'this is how your heavenly Father *** will treat each of you if you do not forgive *** your brother from your heart *** *(hand on heart).'*

THE WIDOW'S OFFERING

Mark 12:41-44; Luke 21:1-4

Teaching point
• giving everything we have to God

Jesus *** *(point upwards)* was sitting *** *(pretend to sit)* in the temple *** *(make a spire shape or point to side of head!)* opposite the place where offerings of money *** *(stroke palm)* were put *** *(shot put!)*. He was watching *** (look at watch) the crowd as they came along *** *(stretch out arms as if measuring)* and put *** their money *** into the treasury box *** *(pretend to box!)*.

Many people came along *** who were rich *** *(say 'loads o' money!')* – very rich *** *(say 'loads an' loads o' money!')*, and as they came to the treasury box *** the rich people *** threw *** *(mime 'through')* large amounts *** *(indicate a large size)* into the box ***, so *** *(sew)* every-one could see *** *(look through binoculars)* how good they were *** *(thumbs up)* and how generous they were *** *(smug sharing-out action)*.

Now a woman whose husband had died *** *(look sad)* came along ***. She was not very rich ***. In fact she was very poor *** *(pour!)*. She only had two *(show 2 fingers)* very small coins *** *(show very tiny circle with thumb and forefinger)* made of copper *** *(bend knees, pull imaginary braces, say 'Evenin' all!')*. She put *** them both into the treasury box ***.

Jesus *** called his disciples to him and said, 'You saw *** *(saw wood)* that widow, she was not very rich *** but she gave everything she had *** *(empty pockets)*. The rich people *** had plenty left over *** *(left arm over!)* when they threw *** their large amounts *** into the treasury box ***. But this widow had nothing *** *(show nought)* left over ***. What she gave was worth much more to God ***.'

ZACCHAEUS

Luke 19:1-10

Teaching points
- salvation
- true repentance
- new life

There was once a man named Zacchaeus *** *(shrink down and sneer)*. Zacchaeus *** was very wicked and evil *** *(wring hands while pulling an evil face)* and he worked for the Roman soldiers *** *(stand to attention)*. He collected *** *(hold out hand flat)* taxes *** *(stroke palm)* from the people *** *(point to everyone)*. Sad to say *** *(pull a sad face)*, Zacchaeus *** took much more money *** *(stroke palm)* than he should have, and he kept it for himself *** *(put money in pocket)*. Because of this, the people *** hated *** *(pull an angry face)* Zacchaeus ***. He had no friends *** *(shake hands with yourself)*.

One day, Zacchaeus *** heard *** *(cup hand round ear)* that Jesus *** *(point upwards)* was coming to his town. He wanted to see *** *(look through binoculars)* Jesus *** very much, but he had one bi . . . g *** *(say 'big' slowly, moving hands outwards to indicate size)* problem *** *(look thoughtful, pointing to side of head)*. Zacchaeus *** was a very small man *** *(indicate short height)*. How would he be able to see *** Jesus ***? There would be so many tall people *** *(stand on tiptoes)* all around *** *(turn around)*. Suddenly *** *(sudden, shocked reaction)* he had a good idea *** *(eyes light up, point to side of head)*. 'I'll climb *** *(climbing action)* a tree *** *(make a tree shape)*,' he thought ***. So *** *(sew)* Zacchaeus *** climbed *** a tree ***. Now he could see *** everything *(point downwards)*, he had a wonderful view *** *(say 'WOW!')*.

Soon Jesus *** came walking *** *(walk on the spot)* towards the tree ***. Suddenly *** Jesus *** stopped *** *(hand signal for stop)*. He looked up *** *(look up)* into the tree *** and said, 'Zacchaeus ***, come down *** *(look downwards)*, for I must come to your house *** *(mime roof)* today'. So *** Jesus *** went to Zacchaeus' *** house *** for tea *** (make a letter T).

Soon Zacchaeus was very sorry *** (shrink down and look sorry) for being so wicked and evil ***. He changed his ways *** (turn around) and gave half *** (mime breaking something in half) his money *** to the poor *** (look downcast) and to those people *** he had robbed *** (grabbing action) he gave back *** (touch back) four *** (show 4 fingers) times as much.

So *** Zacchaeus *** (shrink down and smile!) stopped *** being wicked and evil *** after he had met Jesus ***. HOORAY (all cheer)!